A TAKE - CHARGE GIRL
Blazes a Trail to Congress
The Story of Jeannette Rankin

We're going to vote for JEANNETTE RANKIN & WE HOPE YOU WILL!

JEANNETTE for Congress

Gretchen Woelfle

Illustrated by Rebecca Gibbon

CALKINS CREEK

AN IMPRINT OF ASTRA BOOKS FOR YOUNG READERS

New York

Montana, the Big Sky state—where the mountains rise up to the sky and the plains stretch on forever. Jeannette Rankin rode horses through those mountains and camped under that big sky.

One day a horse came galloping into the Rankins' ranch yard. Its shoulder bled from an ugly gash. Jeannette sprang into action, yelling to the ranch hands to hold the horse steady. She used hot water to clean the wound, then ice to freeze it. Finally, she sewed up the gash with needle and thread.

Jeannette Rankin was a take-charge girl.

At home in Missoula, she helped care for her younger brother and four younger sisters. She rolled up her sleeves to cook for them, sew their clothes, and call the doctor when they were ill.

Most girls in 1900 planned to marry and raise children, but Jeannette wanted a different life.

She went to college and studied mountain snails.
But she couldn't see a future there.

She taught school. That didn't suit her.

She tried sewing dresses and making hats.

That wasn't it either.

In 1907, when she was twenty-seven, Jeannette traveled to San Francisco. There she saw ragged children playing in the streets. They lived in crowded, unhealthy tenements. Their parents worked long hours in dangerous factories.

Could she do something to help?

The Telegraph Hill Neighborhood Center offered child care for babies. After-school clubs for girls and boys. English and citizenship classes for immigrants. A health clinic, garden, playground, and library.

Two women in charge of it all. Women in charge! Jeannette liked that.

She rolled up her sleeves (again!) to help for a few days—and stayed for four months. She took care of the young children and taught them the alphabet.

That gave her a big idea.

She would become a social worker and help improve the lives of poor children and their families.

Jeannette moved to New York City to study social work. Mornings, she attended college classes.

Afternoons, she helped women find jobs and child care.

Every day she saw dreadful hardships. A poor mother abandoned by her husband brought her three small children to Jeannette. She couldn't care for them all, so she asked Jeannette to take her three-year-old boy to an orphanage. It broke Jeannette's heart to send this bright little boy away.

She realized that social workers alone couldn't end such suffering.

But who could?

Lawmakers elected to Congress and state assemblies had that power. They could pass laws to improve housing conditions, health care, and social services for families and children. But lawmakers were men who didn't seem to care about such issues. And only men could vote to elect lawmakers.

"I saw that if we were to have decent laws for children," Jeannette said, **"women would have to vote."**

Now that was a bigger idea!

In 1910 she threw herself into the campaign for women's suffrage—
the right to vote. This movement had been around for more than fifty
years, and a few western states had granted women the vote.

But suffragists wanted *every* American woman to have that right.
Who led the suffrage movement?

WOMEN.

For four years Jeannette crisscrossed the country from New York to California to Florida and back again.

She gave thousands of speeches. She spoke at town halls and factory gates, movie theaters and dance halls.

She organized women's groups to keep talking, printing leaflets, and leading meetings with one message: **Give us the vote!**

Many men—and some women—hated the idea.

They thought women weren't smart enough or tough enough to enter the gritty world of politics.

They thought women should stay home and mind the children.

Jeannette had an answer for them.

It's a woman's place to make a home, but she can't make it if she has no say in the community conditions. It's beautiful and right that a woman should nurse her sick children through typhoid fever, but it's also beautiful and right that she should vote for sanitary measures to prevent that typhoid from spreading.

One night an angry lawmaker hurled a glass of water at Jeannette. She hurled an insult right back, declaring that women would soon vote him out of office.

In 1914, Montana men agreed to hold a vote on women's suffrage. Jeannette went home to take charge. She traveled *six thousand miles* through the mountains and across the plains giving speeches all along the way. She led a mile-long parade at the state fair. Children joined the march, wearing hatbands declaring, "I want my mother to vote."

Jeannette wrote a letter to every voter in Montana: "Women in our organization are from all walks of life. . . . We unite on one point: *we want to vote*."

November 1914—VICTORY!

Jeannette—and all Montana women—could finally vote for a
congressman who would pass bills to help families and children.

But what if . . . Montana elected a CONGRESSWOMAN?!

That was Jeannette's BIGGEST idea yet!

She threw a party and announced . . . *she* would run for Congress.

She expected rousing cheers, but . . . she only heard complaints.

Jeannette had seen what women could do.

It was time they entered the power center of politics—the US Congress.

Fiddlesticks!

She might run for the State Assembly, but NOT for Congress.

You'll NEVER win an election against Men.

Jeannette was just the person to lead the charge. She was the most famous woman in Montana. She had given thousands of speeches. She knew how to organize people. Her brother managed her campaign. Her sisters joined Jeannette Rankin Clubs.

They sent postcards to every woman in the state.

More speeches, more parades.

What did Jeannette pledge to do in Congress?

Sponsor a constitutional amendment to give women the vote in every state.

Sponsor bills to improve labor conditions, housing, and health care for families.

FOR CONGRESS
Jeannette Rankin
REPUBLICAN TICKET
....
NATIONAL WOMAN SUFFRAGE
PROTECTION OF CHILDHOOD
STATE AND NATIONAL PROHIBITION
Look for the name Jeanette Rankin on Ballot
if you don't see it ask the Judge of Elec...

On Tuesday, November 7, 1916, Jeannette voted for the first time—for herself!

Back at home she paced the floor.
Would men vote for a woman?
Would women vote for a woman . . .
or vote at all?
The day ended, the polls closed,
and the ballot count began.
Jeannette still paced.

At one o'clock in the morning she called the
local newspaper.
Was Jeannette Rankin winning?

No, she was losing.

Jeannette collapsed into bed.

On Wednesday the newspaper announced that she had lost. She was crushed until . . . the phone rang and her brother announced that . . . it wasn't over yet!

MONTANA

Votes were still coming in from the countryside and small towns.

Friends came by. Jeannette put on a brave face.
Wednesday, Thursday passed.
Was her biggest idea too big?
Finally on Friday, all the votes were counted and . . .

**Jeannette Rankin became
the first congresswoman ever!**

Rivers of mail flooded in. Rowdy reporters rushed to Montana and demanded a speech. An auto company offered her a new car. A toothpaste company promised her $5,000 to smile in their ads.

Not a chance!

When she finally spoke, she lambasted congressmen who had voted to spend $300,000 to study food for hogs, and only $30,000 to study the needs of children.

She said, "If the hogs of the nation are ten times more important than the children, it is high time that women should make their influence felt."

On April 2, 1917, Jeannette Rankin strode into the Capitol in Washington, DC, to take her seat in the House of Representatives. Her proud family watched from the visitors' gallery. Congressmen rushed to shake her hand. She smiled at each one. But she wasn't there for smiles and handshakes.

She had work to do!

"I may be the first woman member of Congress, but I won't be the last," she declared.

AND SHE WAS RIGHT.

JEANNETTE RANKIN

AUTHOR'S NOTE

Jeannette Rankin wouldn't meet the reporters trampling her front lawn after she won a seat in Congress. But that didn't stop them making up stories about her. This verse by Christopher Morley appeared in the *New York Times* just days after the election. It treated Jeannette's future in Congress as a joke. As for a chaperone, Jeannette certainly didn't need one. She could take care of herself!

The Congresslady

We have so many Congressmen
Whose ways are dark and shady—
How joyfully we welcome then
The coming Congresslady!

I wonder, is she old and stout
Or is she young and pretty?
How long the members will stay out
Who are on her committee!

We'll hear no more of shabbiness
Among our legislators—
She'll make them formal in their dress
They'll wear boiled shirts and gaiters.

Her maiden speeches will be known
For charm and grace of manner;
But who on earth will chaperone
The member from Montana?

Jeannette Rankin, age thirty-six, is pictured here in 1916 during her successful campaign to become the first woman elected to Congress. She loved big stylish hats.

Jeannette Rankin in Congress and Beyond

Congress was the ideal place for Jeannette Rankin. She could use her boundless energy, fierce determination, and public-speaking skills to work for change. She always voted her conscience, even if she made enemies—which she did. She kept her promise to work for women and children, but she was a woman ahead of her time. Many of the measures that she supported only became law after she left Congress. However her achievements include:

- She was the first member of Congress to hire an all-woman office staff.
- She cosponsored a health bill for women and children.
- She cosponsored a bill against child labor.
- She introduced a bill calling for equal pay for men and women.
- She supported a bill for a constitutional amendment for women's suffrage.
- She supported women workers in organizing a union at the Bureau of Printing and Engraving in Washington, DC.
- She cast her first vote against bringing the United States into World War I. She was vilified for it. In later years she said, "I felt at the time that the first woman [in Congress] should take the first stand, that the first time the first woman had a chance to say no to war she should say it."
- When war was declared, she voted for military bills in order to end the war quickly.
- She voted against bills that limited free speech in wartime.

Jeannette Rankin was not reelected in 1918 because of her unpopular vote against the war. She spent the next two decades working for peace and social welfare.

In 1940 she was reelected to Congress and worked to keep America out of the war in Europe. When Japan attacked Pearl Harbor in December 1941, President Franklin Roosevelt asked Congress to declare war. Rankin, an unwavering pacifist, was the only member of Congress to vote against entering World War II.

Senator John F. Kennedy, who later became president, wrote of her 1941 vote against war in a magazine article, "Three Women of Courage":

> Few members of Congress since its founding in 1789 have ever stood more alone, more completely in defiance of popular opinion, than former Representative Jeannette Rankin of Montana. . . . Most of us do not associate the quality of courage with women in public affairs. We neither expect it nor reward it.

In her final years Jeannette Rankin came out of retirement to campaign against the war in Vietnam. In 1968, when she was eighty-seven, she led a peace march of five thousand women in Washington, DC. The marchers called themselves the Jeannette Rankin Brigade.

And the trail she blazed to Congress? Since Jeannette's victory in 1916, 397 women have served in Congress, including 94 women of color. In 2022, 24 women served in the US Senate, 125 served in the House of Representatives, and one as vice president. In addition, women are elected to office at all levels, from city councils and mayors to state legislatures and governors. And the White House? We're still waiting. It won't be long now.

JEANNETTE RANKIN TIMELINE

1880 June 11: JR born in Grant Creek, Montana.

1889 Montana becomes the forty-first state.

1898 JR enters Montana State University in Missoula.

1902 JR graduates with a BA in biology.

1907 JR visits San Francisco; works in a settlement house.

1908 JR enters the New York School of Philanthropy (now the Columbia University School of Social Work); graduates in 1909.

1909 JR works at Spokane, Washington, Children's Home Society.

1910 JR volunteers for Washington state suffrage campaign; November: women win the vote in Washington state.

1910–1914 JR campaigns across the US for National American Woman Suffrage Association.

1911 February 1: JR speaks to Montana legislature on women's suffrage.

1913 March 3: Women's suffrage parade of five thousand held in Washington, DC; JR marches with Montana delegation.

1914 August: World War I declared in Europe.

1914 JR returns to Montana for women's suffrage campaign; travels six thousand miles speaking and organizing; November 3: women's suffrage passes.

1916 JR runs for Congress on Republican ticket in Montana; November 7: elected the first US congresswoman.

1917 April 2: JR takes her seat in Congress; President Woodrow Wilson asks for declaration of war to enter World War I; April 6: JR votes against the war.

1918 November: JR loses election to the US Senate; World War I ends.

1919 JR travels to Switzerland for the meeting of the International Committee of Women for Permanent Peace; visits war-torn France; Treaty of Versailles punishes Germany harshly.

1920 Nineteenth Amendment to the US Constitution becomes law, giving all US women the vote.

1920–1924 JR lobbies for labor and family issues.

1924–1939 JR works for peace groups, traveling and speaking, as well as lobbying in Washington, DC.

1933 Nazi Party leader Adolf Hitler becomes chancellor of Germany.

1937 JR visits Germany and sees military buildup.

1939 World War II begins: Germany invades Poland; England and France declare war.

1940 JR runs for Congress in Montana on a peace platform; wins November election.

1941 December 7: Japan attacks Pearl Harbor; December 8: President Franklin D. Roosevelt asks Congress for declaration of war; JR casts the only vote against it.

1943 JR returns to Montana when her term in Congress ends.

1945 Germany and Japan surrender, ending World War II.

1946–70 JR travels to India seven times and to Asia, Africa, Europe, and Latin America.

1961 JR awarded honorary doctorate of laws degree from Montana State College.

1961 President John F. Kennedy sends military advisers to Vietnam to assist South Vietnamese Army against North Vietnam.

1965 US combat troops sent to Vietnam; antiwar demonstrations held all across US; JR joins the protests.

1968 January 15: The five thousand women of the Jeannette Rankin Brigade protest the Vietnam War.

1968–73 JR speaks out against the war at colleges, rallies, and on television.

1970 June 11: JR's ninetieth birthday party held in Washington, DC; celebrated by past and present politicians.

1972 Honored as "the world's outstanding living feminist" and first member of the Susan B. Anthony Hall of Fame

1973 January 27: Peace treaty signed, ending US role in the Vietnam War;

May 18: JR dies peacefully in Carmel, California.

On April 2, 1916, her first day in Congress, Jeannette Rankin addressed her supporters from the balcony of the National American Woman Suffrage Association (NAWSA) in Washington, DC. Behind her stands Carrie Chapman Catt, president of NAWSA, who often quarreled with Jeannette.

In 1939, Jeannette Rankin, a committed pacifist, was appalled by the buildup of the US military in response to threats of war from Japan and Germany. She appeared before a congressional committee to express her views. Though fashions had changed, she still sported a stylish hat.

RESEARCH BIBLIOGRAPHY

All quotations used in the book can be found in the following sources marked with an asterisk (*).

Giles, Kevin S. *Flight of the Dove: The Story of Jeannette Rankin*. Beaverton, OR: Touchstone Press, 1980.

Harris, Ted C. *Jeannette Rankin: Suffragist, First Woman Elected to Congress, and Pacifist*. New York: Arno Press, 1982.

*"If the hopes of the nation . . .": Jeanette Rankin, *New York Sunday American*, November 26, 1916.

*Josephson, Hannah. *Jeannette Rankin, First Lady in Congress: A Biography*. Indianapolis: Bobbs-Merrill, 1974.

*Kennedy, John F. "Three Women of Courage." *McCall's Magazine*, January 1958: 36–37, 54–55.

Lopach, James J., and Jean A. Luckowski. *Jeannette Rankin: A Political Woman*. Boulder: University Press of Colorado, 2005.

*Mallon, Winifred. "An Impression of Jeannette Rankin." *The Suffragist*, March 31, 1917: n.p.

*Morley, Christopher. "The Congress Lady." *New York Times Sunday Magazine*, November 19, 1916.

*Smith, Norma. *Jeannette Rankin: America's Conscience*. Helena: Montana Historical Society Press, 2002.

Books for Young Readers

Conkling, Winifred. *Votes for Women! American Suffragists and The Battle for the Ballot*. Chapel Hill, NC: Algonquin Young Readers: 2018.

O'Brien, Mary Barmeyer. *Jeannette Rankin, 1880–1973: Bright Star in the Big Sky*. Helena, MT: Falcon Press, 1995.

Woelfle, Gretchen. *Jeannette Rankin: Political Pioneer*. Honesdale, PA: Boyds Mills/Calkins Creek, 2007.

Websites*

Biography of Rankin with links to her work in Congress, The Jeannette Rankin Foundation. rankinfoundation.org. Awards scholarships to low-income women over thirty-five.

History, Art, and Archives of the US House of Representatives. history.house.gov/People/Listing/R/RANKIN,-Jeannette-(R000055).

Jeannette Rankin interviews, 1972, University of California, Berkeley Oral History Center. calisphere.org/item/ark:/13030/kt758005dx. Many hours of lively interviews with Rankin recounting her life story.

National Women's Hall of Fame. womenofthehall.org/inductee/jeannette-rankin. Features a short biography of Jeannette Rankin.

The Jeannette Rankin Peace Center. jrpc.org. The center's mission is "to connect and empower people to build a socially just, non-violent and sustainable community and world."

*Websites active at time of publication

ACKNOWLEDGMENTS

As more and more women are elected to public offices, it seems perfectly natural that they should be there. But it took people like Jeannette Rankin to break down the prejudices that kept women out of politics. I thank Carolyn Yoder for her editorial prowess and her unflagging enthusiasm for Jeannette Rankin. Historian Joan Hoff generously reviewed the manuscript for me. My esteemed writers' group—Alexis O'Neill, Caroline Arnold, Ann Stampler, and Sherrill Kushner—having read multiple drafts of this book, know (and love) Jeannette nearly as well as I do. Thanks also to Kerry McManus, Barbara Grzeslo, and the rest of the staff at Calkins Creek/Astra Books for Young Readers for their help in bringing this book to life. I've been a fan of Rebecca Gibbon's art for many years now, and am honored to share Jeannette's story with her.

This statue of Jeannette Rankin stands in Emancipation Hall, U.S. Capitol Visitors Center, Washington, DC. A replica stands in the state capitol in Helena, Montana. Women state legislators have been known to rub Jeannette's foot before entering the legislative halls.

To Elizabeth Morrison, a true friend and a good writer —*GW*
For Cate, my biggest fan —*RG*

PICTURE CREDITS

Calkins Creek
An Imprint of Astra Books for Young Readers, a division of Astra Publishing House
astrapublishinghouse.com
Printed in China

ISBN: 978-1-6626-8012-0 (hc)
ISBN: 978-1-6626-8013-7 (eBook)
Library of Congress Control Number: 2021925700

First edition
10 9 8 7 6 5 4 3 2 1

Design by Barbara Grzeslo
The text is set in Frutiger LT Std 45 Light.
The art is done with acrylic inks & colored pencil on acid-free cartridge paper.